The ABCs of Salvation

M. R. Dayce

Published by Passion Publications
a division of
Tell the Truth International
7005 Woodbine Ave
Sacramento, Ca. 95822
tellthetruthsac@gmail.com

Printed in the United States of America
© 2021 by Melodie Dayce

All rights reserved. No part of this book may be reproduced in whole or part, in any form or by any means, electronic or mechanical, including photocopying, recording or by any information storage and retrieval system without express written permission from the author.

Scripture quotations marked KJV are taken from the King James Version of the Bible.

Scripture quotations marked (AMPCE) are taken from the Amplified Bible, Copyright c 1954, 1958, 1962, 1964, 1965, 1987 by The Lockman Foundation. Used by permission.

Scripture quotations marked (NIV) are taken from the Holy Bible, New International Version®, NIV®. Copyright © 1973, 1978, 1984, 2011 by Biblica, Inc.™ Used by permission of Zondervan. All rights reserved worldwide. www.zondervan.com The "NIV" and "New International Version" are trademarks registered in the United States Patent and Trademark Office by Biblica, Inc.™

ISBN: 978-1-957101-00-2

God loves you! You know He gave us the ABCs to help us learn to read and write; He also gave us the ABCs of Salvation.

Jesus paid the price for all of our sins; past, present and future. This is a basic guide of the actions we need to grow in our relationship with God.

Our actions show our love and appreciation for what Jesus did for us.

The numbered references given on some pages refer to the Strongest Strong's Exhaustive Concordance of the Bible – By James Strong. Fully revised and corrected by John R. Kohnlenberger III and James A. Swanson, 2001

A is for **Accept**

Accept Jesus as your Savior.

Romans 6:23 KJV	For the wages of sin is death, but the gift of god is eternal life through Jesus Christ our Lord.
	When we accept Jesus Christ as our Savior we are adopted into God's royal family.
Ephesians1:5 NIV	He predestined us to be adopted as his sons through Jesus Christ, in accordance with his pleasure and will.

B is for **Believe**

Believe that Jesus is the Son of God.

John 3:16 NIV	For God so loved the world that he gave his one and only Son, that whoever believes in him shall not perish but have eternal life.
KJV	For God so loved the world that he gave his only begotten Son, that whosoever believeth in him should not perish, but have everlasting life.

C is for **Confess**

Confess Jesus as your Lord and Savior.

Romans 10:9,10 NIV	That if you confess with your mouth "Jesus is Lord," and believe in your heart that God raised him from the dead, you will be saved. For it is with your heart that you believe and are justified (or declared righteous), and it is with your mouth that you confess and are saved.
KJV	That if thou shalt confess with thy mouth the Lord Jesus, and shalt believe in thine heart that God hath raised him from the dead, thou shalt be saved. For with the heart man believeth unto righteousness, and with the mouth confession is made unto salvation.

D is for Doer

James 1:22 KJV	But be ye doers of the word, and not hearers only, deceiving your own selves.
AMPCE	But be doers of the Word (obey the message), and not merely listeners to it, betraying yourselves (into deception by reasoning contrary to the Truth).

E is for **Endure**

2 Timothy 2:3,4 NIV	Endure hardship with us like a good soldier of Jesus Christ. No one serving as a soldier gets involved in civilian affairs - he wants to please his commanding officer.
KJV	Thou therefore endure hardness, as a good soldier of Jesus Christ. No man that warreth entangleth himself with the affairs of this life; that he may please him who hath chosen him to be a soldier.

F is for **Forgive**

Mark 11:25 AMPCE	And whenever you stand praying, if you have anything against anyone, forgive him and let it drop (leave it, let it go), in order that your Father Who is in heaven may also forgive you your [own] failings and shortcomings and let it go.
KJV	And when ye stand praying, forgive, if ye have aught against any: that your Father also which is in heaven may forgive you your trespasses.

G is for **Grow**

2 Peter 3:18 KJV	But grow in grace, and in the knowledge of our Lord and Saviour Jesus Christ. To him be glory both now and forever. Amen

Strong's Greek #5485	–	grace: the state of kindness and favor towards someone, often with a focus on a benefit given to the object.

H is for **Humble**

Luke 11:14 NIV	For everyone who exalts himself will be humbled, and he who humbles himself will be exalted.
James 4:10 KJV	Humble yourselves in the sight of the Lord, and he shall lift you up.

Strong's Greek #5013 — humble: to humble oneself, lower oneself, brought low.

I is for **Imitator**

Ephesians 5:1 AMPCE	Therefore be imitators of God (copy Him and follow His example), as well-beloved children (imitate their father).
NIV	Be imitators of God, therefore as dearly loved children.

J is for **Joyful**

Psalms 63:5 AMPCE	My whole being shall be satisfied with marrow and fatness; and my mouth shall praise You with joyful lips.
Psalms 100:1 KJV	Make a joyful noise unto the Lord, all ye lands.

K is for **Kind**

Ephesians 4:32 KJV

And be ye kind one to another, tenderhearted, forgiving one another, even as God for Christ's sake hath forgiven you.

L is for **Love**

Jesus shared the Great Commandment

Mark 12:30,31 NIV	Love the Lord your God with all your heart and with all your soul and with all your mind and with all your strength. The second is this: Love your neighbor as yourself. There is no commandment greater than these.
KJV	And thou shalt love the Lord thy God with all thy heart, and with all thy soul, and with all thy mind, and with all thy strength: this is the first commandment. And the second is like, namely this, thou shalt love thy neighbor as thyself. There is none other commandment greater than these.

M is for **Magnify**

Psalms 34:3 O magnify the Lord with
KJV me, let us exalt his name
together.

N is for **Near**

Hebrews 10:22 NIV	Let us draw near to God with a sincere heart in full assurance of faith, having our hearts sprinkled to cleanse us from a guilty conscience and having our bodies washed with pure water.
KJV	Let us draw near with a true heart in full assurance of faith, having our hearts sprinkled from an evil conscience, and our bodies washed with pure water.

O is for **Occupy**

Luke 19:13 KJV

And he called his ten servants, and delivered them ten pounds, and said unto them, Occupy till I come.

Strong's Greek #4231 — occupy: to put capital to work, do business.

P is for **Pray**

Matthew 26:41 KJV	Watch and pray, that ye enter not into temptation: the spirit is indeed willing, but the flesh is weak.
1 Thessalonians 5:17 KJV	Pray without ceasing.

Q is for **Quiet**

1 Timothy 2:1,2 KJV	I exhort therefore, that, first of all, supplications, prayers, intercessions, and giving of thanks, be made to all men; For kings, and for all that are in authority; that we may lead a quiet and peaceable life in all godliness and honesty.
AMPCE	First of all then, I admonish and urge that petitions, prayers, intercessions, and thanksgivings be offered on behalf of all men, for kings and all who are in positions of authority or high responsibility, that (outwardly) we may pass a quiet and undisturbed life (and inwardly) a peaceable one in all godliness and reverence and seriousness in every way.

R is for **Rooted**

Colossians 2:6-7 NIV	So then, just as you received Christ Jesus as Lord, continue to live in him, rooted and built up in him, strengthened in the faith as you were taught, overflowing with thankfulness.
KJV	As ye have therefore received Christ Jesus the Lord, so walk ye in him: Rooted and built up in him, and stablished in the faith, as ye have been taught, abounding therein with thanksgiving.

Strong's Greek #4491 — rooted: to be rooted, with the associative meaning that a rooted object is strong and healthy.

S is for Study

2 Timothy 2:15 KJV	Study to show thyself approved unto God, a workman that needeth not to be ashamed, rightly dividing the word of truth.
AMPCE	Study and be eager and do your utmost to present yourself to God approved (tested by trial), a workman who has no cause to be ashamed, correctly analyzing and accurately dividing (rightly handling and skillfully teaching) the Word of Truth.

T is for **Thanks**

1 Thessalonians 5:18 KJV	In everything give thanks: for this is the will of God in Christ Jesus concerning you.
NIV	Give thanks in all circumstances, for this is God's will for you in Christ Jesus.

U is for **Understanding**

1 Corinthians 14:20 KJV	Brethren, be not children in understanding: howbeit in malice be ye children, but in understanding be men.
AMPCE	Brethren, do not be children (immature) in thinking: continue to be babes in (matters of) evil, but in your minds be mature men.

Strong's Greek #5424 — understanding: thinking

V is for **Vigilant**

1 Peter 5:8 KJV	Be sober, be vigilant; because your adversary the devil, as a roaring lion, walketh about, seeking whom he may devour.
NIV	Be self-controlled and alert. Your enemy the devil prowls around like a roaring lion looking for someone to devour.

Strong's Greek #1127 — vigilant: to keep watch, be on guard.

W is for **Work**

John 9:4 KJV	I must work the works of him that sent me, while it is day: the night cometh, when no man can work.
AMPCE	We must work the works of Him Who sent Me and be busy with His business while it is daylight; night is coming on, when no man can work.

Strong's Greek #2038 — work: be active, accomplish something.

X is for **Exhort**

Hebrews 3:13　　But exhort one another daily, while it is called Today; lest any of you be hardened through the deceitfulness of sin.
KJV

Y is for **Yield**

Romans 6:13 KJV	Neither yield ye your members as instruments of unrighteousness unto sin: but yield yourselves unto God, as those that are alive from the dead, and your members as instruments of righteousness unto God.
AMPCE	Do not continue offering or yielding your bodily members (and faculties) to sin as instruments (tools) of wickedness.
	But offer and yield yourselves to God as though you have been raised from the dead to (perpetual) life, and your bodily members (and faculties) to God, presenting them as implements of righteousness.

Strong's Greek #3936 — yield: to present, make an offering.

Z is for **Zealous**

1 Corinthians 14:12 KJV	Even so ye, forasmuch as ye are zealous of spiritual gifts, seek that ye may excel to the edifying of the church.
NIV	So it is with you, since you are eager to have spiritual gifts, try to excel in gifts that build up the church.

Strong's Greek #2207	–	zealous: zealot, enthusiast, one who has the feelings or attitudes of deep commitment to a person or cause.

Prayer to Receive Jesus As Your Savior

This is the most important decision you'll ever make – choosing to receive Jesus as your Lord and Savior!

God's word says, "If thou shalt confess with thy mouth the Lord Jesus, and shalt believe in thine heart that God hath raised him from the dead, thou shalt be saved. For with the heart man believeth unto righteousness; and with the mouth confession is made unto salvation.

Romans 10:9,10

Now pray out loud, "Jesus, I come to you right now. I accept you as Lord and Savior over my life. I believe in my heart that you are the Son of God, and that you died and rose from the dead for my salvation. I repent of sin. I confess with my mouth that Jesus Is Lord! Thank you for saving me today – I am a child of Almighty God!"

God you said in Luke 11:13, "...how much more shall your heavenly Father give the Holy Spirit to them that ask?" I am asking you right now to fill me with the Holy Spirit so I will have your power to live this new life. As I praise God, Holy Spirit rise up in me, I receive you by faith right now!

Find a Bible believing church that teaches the word of God and fellow-ship with other believers. Pray, read, and obey the word of God so you will know Him and grow in His character. Receive water baptism (Matthew 3:6) as a witness of your new life in Christ.

www.ingramcontent.com/pod-product-compliance
Lightning Source LLC
Chambersburg PA
CBHW021433070526
44577CB00001B/183